THE SEATTLE SEAHAWKS

BY ALICIA Z. KLEPEIS

★ NFL ★ TEAM PROFILES

EPIC

BELLWETHER MEDIA ★ MINNEAPOLIS, MN

EPIC BOOKS are no ordinary books. They burst with intense action, high-speed heroics, and shadows of the unknown. Are you ready for an Epic adventure?

This edition first published in 2024 by Bellwether Media, Inc.

Library of Congress Cataloging-in-Publication Data

Names: Klepeis, Alicia, 1971- author.
Title: The Seattle Seahawks / by Alicia Z. Klepeis.
Description: Minneapolis, MN : Bellwether Media, 2024. | Series: Epic. NFL team profiles | Includes bibliographical references and index. | Audience: Ages 7-12 | Audience: Grades 2-3 | Summary: "Engaging images accompany information about the Seattle Seahawks. The combination of high-interest subject matter and light text is intended for students in grades 2 through 7"-- Provided by publisher.
Identifiers: LCCN 2023021972 (print) | LCCN 2023021973 (ebook) | ISBN 9798886874945 (library binding) | ISBN 9798886876826 (ebook)
Subjects: LCSH: Seattle Seahawks (Football team)--History--Juvenile literature.
Classification: LCC GV956.S4 K54 2024 (print) | LCC GV956.S4 (ebook) | DDC 796.332/6409797772--dc23/eng/20230517
LC record available at https://lccn.loc.gov/2023021972
LC ebook record available at https://lccn.loc.gov/2023021973

Editor: Kieran Downs Designer: Josh Brink

Printed in the United States of America, North Mankato, MN.

TABLE OF CONTENTS

A WILD CARD WIN

The Seahawks face the Eagles in the 2019 **playoffs**. The game is tied 3–3.

Running back Marshawn Lynch runs for 5 yards. He spins and jumps into the **end zone**. The **touchdown** helps the Seahawks win the game!

MARSHAWN LYNCH

THE HISTORY OF THE SEAHAWKS

The Seahawks played their first season in Seattle, Washington, in 1976. They were an **expansion team** in the National Football League (NFL).

Quarterback Jim Zorn was an early star. So was **wide receiver** Steve Largent. The team had a winning record by their third year!

STEVE LARGENT

JIM ZORN

NAME GAME

The Seahawks held a contest to decide their name in 1975. It was won by Hazel Cooke. She won two 1976 season tickets!

CHUCK KNOX

1983 AFC CHAMPIONSHIP GAME

Chuck Knox became the team's head coach in 1983. The Seahawks made it to the AFC **Championship** Game that season. But the Los Angeles Raiders beat them.

The team reached the playoffs three more times in the 1980s!

1984 PLAYOFF GAME

The Seahawks struggled in the 1990s. But running back Shaun Alexander helped the team in the 2000s. They reached the playoffs five years in a row!

SHAUN ALEXANDER

SUPER BOWL 40

The Seahawks made it to their first **Super Bowl** in 2006. But they lost to the Pittsburgh Steelers.

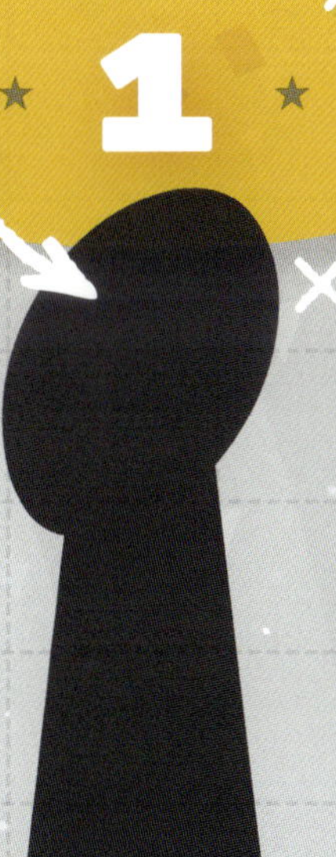

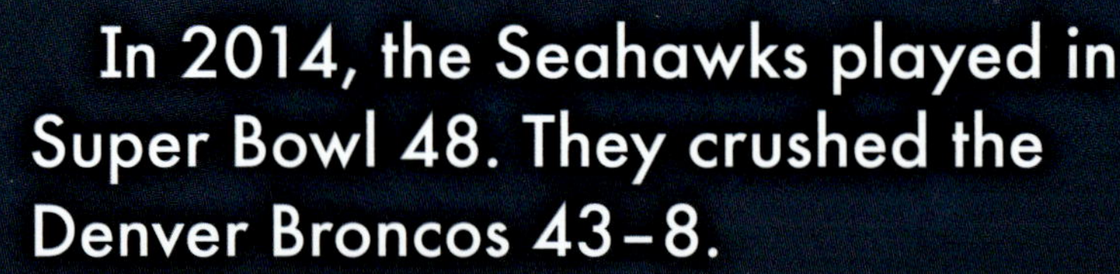

In 2014, the Seahawks played in Super Bowl 48. They crushed the Denver Broncos 43–8.

TOP TEAMMATES

Wide receiver Doug Baldwin scored touchdowns in Super Bowls 48 and 49. He caught passes from Russell Wilson both times.

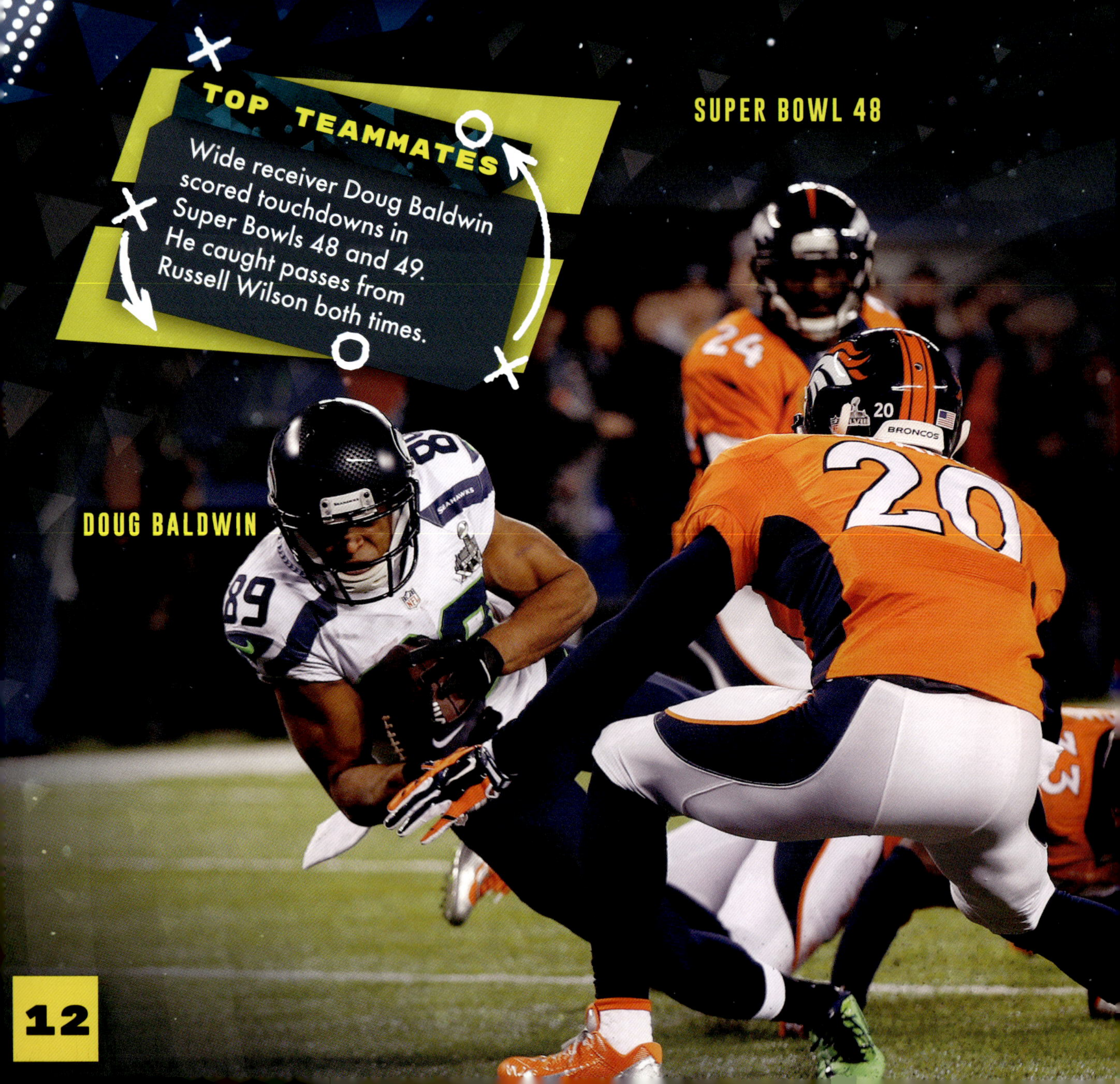

SUPER BOWL 48

DOUG BALDWIN

The team returned to the Super Bowl the next year. But they lost to the New England Patriots. The team hopes for another chance soon.

SUPER BOWL 49

THE SEAHAWKS TODAY

SEAHAWKS VS. 49ERS

The Seahawks play home games at Lumen Field. It is in Seattle, Washington.

The team plays in the NFC West. The San Francisco 49ers are their biggest **rival**. Another is the Los Angeles Rams.

ONE HUGE ROOF

Lumen Field has a huge roof. It is 760 feet (232 meters) long. That is about as long as three Boeing 747 airplanes lined up end to end!

LOCATION

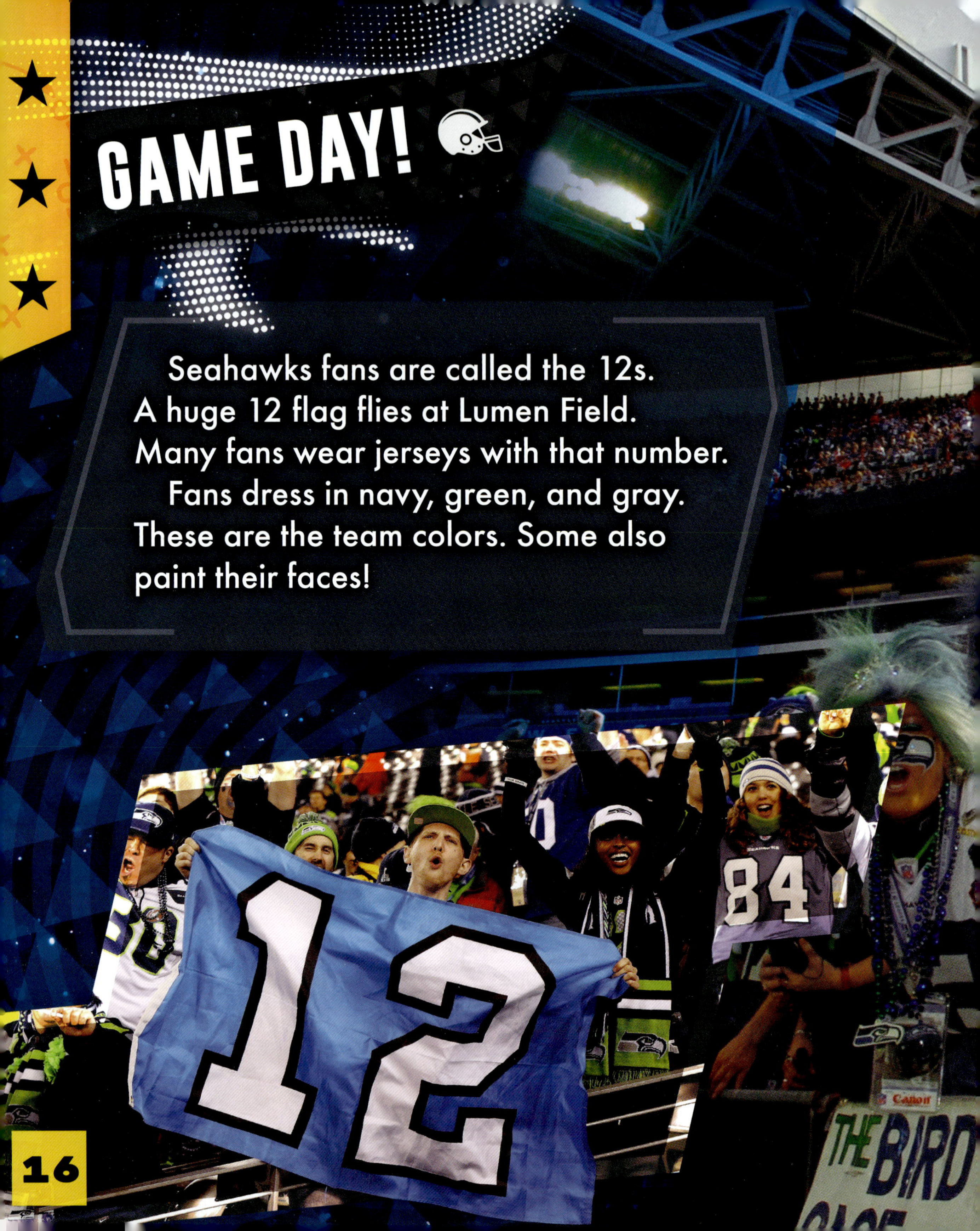

GAME DAY!

Seahawks fans are called the 12s. A huge 12 flag flies at Lumen Field. Many fans wear jerseys with that number.

Fans dress in navy, green, and gray. These are the team colors. Some also paint their faces!

BEAST QUAKE

In 2011, Marshawn Lynch ran for a 67-yard touchdown. Fans cheered so loudly that it caused an earthquake detector to go off!

Blitz and Boom are the team's **mascots**. They dance with fans on game days.

A live hawk named Taima flies around the field before games. It gets fans excited. The 12s cheer for the Seahawks throughout the season!

★ FAMOUS PLAYERS ★

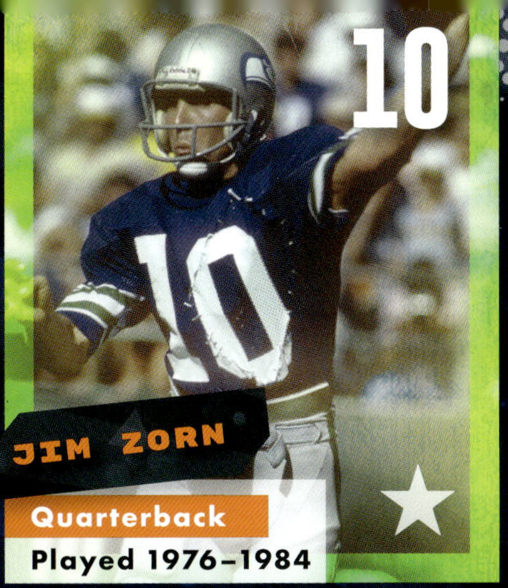

JIM ZORN

Quarterback

Played 1976–1984

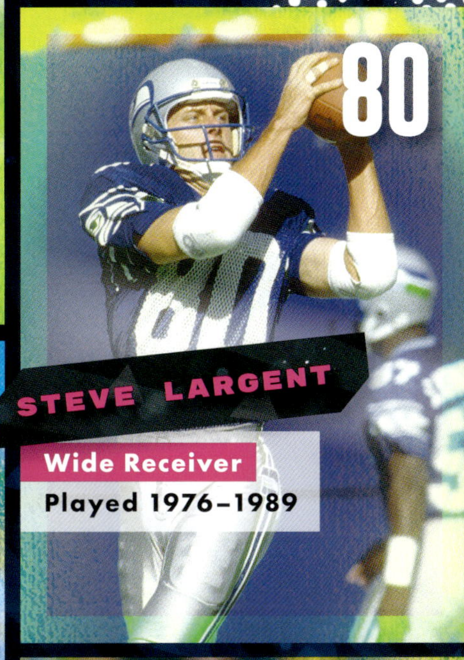

STEVE LARGENT

Wide Receiver

Played 1976–1989

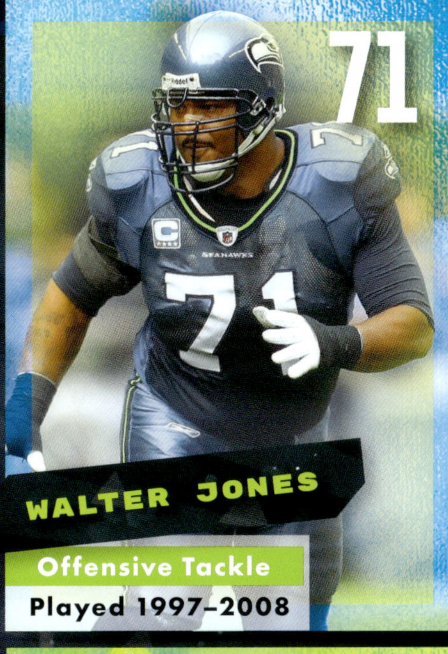

WALTER JONES

Offensive Tackle

Played 1997–2008

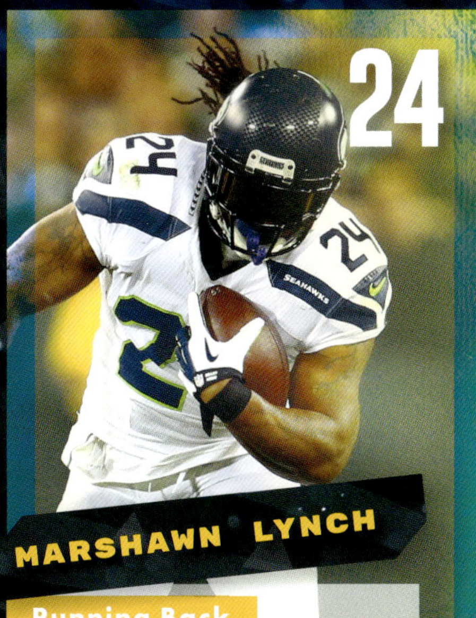

MARSHAWN LYNCH

Running Back

Played 2010–2015, 2019

RUSSELL WILSON

Quarterback

Played 2012–2021

SEATTLE SEAHAWKS FACTS

LOGO

JOINED THE NFL | 1976

NICKNAME | The Hawks

MASCOTS

CONFERENCE

National Football Conference (NFC)

COLORS

DIVISION | NFC West

Arizona Cardinals

Los Angeles Rams

San Francisco 49ers

STADIUM

LUMEN FIELD

opened July 28, 2002

holds **68,740** people

TIMELINE

1976
The Seahawks play their first season

1983
The Seahawks win their first playoff game

2006
The Seahawks play in Super Bowl 40

2014
The Seahawks win Super Bowl 48

2015
The Seahawks play in Super Bowl 49

 RECORDS 

All-Time Passing Leader
Russell Wilson
37,059 yards

All-Time Rushing Leader
Shaun Alexander
9,429 yards

All-Time Receiving Leader
Steve Largent
13,089 yards

All-Time Scoring Leader
Norm Johnson
810 points

GLOSSARY

championship—a contest to decide the best team or person

end zone—an area at either end of a football field; teams score points when they go into the end zone.

expansion team—a new team added to a sports league

mascots—animals or symbols that represent a sports team

playoffs—games played after the regular season is over; playoff games determine which teams play in the championship game.

quarterback—a player whose main job is to throw and hand off the ball

rival—a long-standing opponent

running back—a player whose main job is to run with the ball

Super Bowl—the annual championship game of the NFL

touchdown—a score that occurs when a team crosses into their opponent's end zone with the football; a touchdown is worth six points.

wide receiver—a player whose main job is to catch passes from the quarterback

TO LEARN MORE

AT THE LIBRARY

Fishman, Jon M. *Russell Wilson.* Minneapolis, Minn.: Lerner Publications, 2021.

Storm, Marysa. *Highlights of the Seattle Seahawks.* Mankato, Minn.: Black Rabbit Books, 2020.

Whiting, Jim. *The Story of the Seattle Seahawks.* Minneapolis, Minn.: Kaleidoscope, 2020.

ON THE WEB

FACTSURFER

Factsurfer.com gives you a safe, fun way to find more information.

1. Go to www.factsurfer.com.
2. Enter "Seattle Seahawks" into the search box and click 🔍.
3. Select your book cover to see a list of related content.

INDEX

The images in this book are reproduced through the courtesy of: Stephen Brashear, cover (hero); Paparacy, cover (stadium); David Eulitt/ Getty, p. 3; Steven Ryan/ Getty, p. 4; Icon Sportswire/ Getty, pp. 5, 20 (Blitz), 21 (2014); Damian Strohmeyer/ Getty, p. 6; Diamond Images/ AP Images, pp. 6-7; Anonymous/ AP Images, p. 8; Focus On Sport, pp. 8 (Chuck Knox), 19 (Jim Zorn, Steve Largent), 21 (Steve Largent); George Gojkovich/ Getty, p. 9; Rob Tringali/ Getty, p. 10; Kevin C. Cox/ Getty, p. 12; Stephen Dunn/ Getty, p. 13; Michael Zagaris/ Getty, p. 14; Ian Dewar/ Alamy, p. 15; NFL/ Wikipedia, pp. 15 (Seahawks logo), 20 (Seahawks logo, Cardinals logo, Rams logo, 49ers logo, NFC logo); Christian Petersen/ Getty, pp. 16, 21 (2015); Kirby Lee/ AP Images, pp. 16-17; Ted S. Warren/ AP Images. pp. 18-19 (Blitz); Tom Hauck/ Getty, p. 18 (Taima); Otto Greule Jr/ Getty, pp. 19 (Walter Jones, Russell Wilson), 21 (Shaun Alexander); Maddie Meyer, p. 19 (Marshawn Lynch); AB Forces News Collection/ Alamy, p. 20 (Boom); Jeremy Graham/ Alamy, p. 20 (stadium); Vernon Biever/ AP Images, p. 21 (1976); Jeff Larson/ AP Images, p. 21 (1983); Mike Ehrmann/ Getty, p. 21 (2006); ZUMA Press/ Alamy, p. 21 (Russell Wilson); Owen C. Shaw/ Getty, p. 21 (Norm Johnson); Grindstone Media Group, p. 23.